The Room Where Summer Ends

Peter Cooley

Carnegie-Mellon University Press
Pittsburgh & London 1979

For Jacqueline

ACKNOWLEDGMENTS

Acknowledgment is gratefully made to editors
of the following magazines in which most of
these poems first appeared:

*California Quarterly, The Chariton Review,
The Georgia Review, Hiram Poetry Review,
Ironwood, The Louisville Review, The Midwest
Quarterly, The Missouri Review, The New
Laurel Review, New Orleans Review, The New
Republic, Northwest Review, Open Places,
Poetry, Poetry Northwest, Poetry Now,
The Ponchartrain Review, Porch, Quarterly
West, Southern Poetry Review, The Southern
Review, Three Rivers Poetry Journal, Uzzano,*
and *The Virginia Quarterly Review.*

"Ararat" first appeared in *The Georgia Review,*
Fall, 1978. *"Skywritings"* is Reprinted by
Permission of *The New Republic,* copyright 1975,
The New Republic, Inc. *"Observances", "From
the Gulf", "An Exorcism",* and *"Conclusion
of a Letter to the Angel"* first appeared in *Poetry.*

The author wishes to thank the Corporation at Yaddo, where
some of these poems were written, and the Tulane University
Graduate School for two summer grants which allowed for
the writing of poems and the preparation of this manuscript.

Library of Congress Catalog Card Number 79-51605
ISBN 0-915604-27-2
ISBN 0-915604-28-0 pbk.

*The publication of this book is supported by grants from the
National Endowment for the Arts in Washington, D.C., a Federal
agency, and from the Pennsylvania Council on the Arts.*

CONTENTS

OBSERVANCES

OBSERVANCES

The cloud cover has blown over.
Now before the bamboo grove
gnats fasten on the noon
like a sudden shower in sunlight
knitting the garden where I lie
releasing them into their stitches, swarming.

When I speak it will be evening.
I'll wait here, wrapped in light
watching stars thicken between leaves
around the moon, numberless, reflecting:
somewhere in the other lives
I came towards myself myself,
a dog barking after dark, a nightjar,
a bevy of flies at the screen door.

Noon. I lie under the gnats
taking the sutures in my skin
to count these wounds my own,
nobody to sing to, mute,
but each little god I can make up
calling him Peter, Peter, Peter,
Peter, Peter, & knowing he never comes.

RETURN

Now at your first word
this landscape is dissolving
into deep gold, haze
your eyes can steady on. Steady,
the far fields squat & stretch
rounding toward summer;
lake flies film your stare.

And here you are:
another spring torn off
your life asking you nothing —
the thorn tree shaped by winter
into an angel's wing turned back
into a thorn tree in white heat
& the little gods crawl up into the air.

DANDELIONS

Once I knew what dying was
in a field run wild with thousands
going to seed. I stood there, dumb,
at the edge of town, myself,
where May was what the earth gave up
to clouds, cloudless, & summer kept the wind
that hadn't risen yet. I waited,

twelve years old. I stand here even now,
stripping off my clothes, going down
naked on my knees, shaking, shaking
their lives away, their heads
fireworks of skulls in the last fire
turning finally to snow, turning to air.
This is how the blessed will rise I think

years later, but this day nothing
human or in images can touch me,
pushing their heads against the sun,
multiplying the field, the road
to town, until I find just one in bloom
& then before I dress & turn back home
rub all my body gold, losing the world.

PRODIGAL

You had walked out, carrying the rain
lightly over your shoulder
on this path you cut through coming home;
you had taken rocks, the ground itself
& wiped your name from them:
holystone, you said, *holystone,*
rhyming the echo, the echo, the echo.

You had called yourself the last star
in your father's eyes, the bright one
nobody could put out. You stood
where the sky stopped turning forever
whenever you caught his stare.
Then your brother's found you, narrowed,
& shot up, a sleek, expensive tree

twining his roots under the house.
Just to think of it you shuddered
packing up your room while mother
went about the business of mothers
with your brother's limbs circling your father
till you stood mute at the door.
But already you were somebody else

suffering the cage, the rich, stiff smell
of yourself, your fights nightly
& the ditches of women, that molten lead
every sky turned toward without a word —
so now tonight the branches thicken, bristling
a whole past you push back at the gate
making your return absurdly difficult,

& vines crawl underfoot reminding you
how deep your leaving was, and snakes
rise at either side while you begin to sing
goodbye, goodbye, this time without words
for the house, his now, standing in the moon
& your brother's face catching the light
erect, lifting how far it took you to get here.

CONCLUSION OF A LETTER TO THE ANGEL

What I'm trying to get down is
I'm excited by this body of mine
following me around, hunkering
over women, the heft & tuft
breathing & urges lift
over my life, a hairy circumstance.

Why don't you answer these letters?

You could press me to your breast
in fire & yet you drive me out
with your silence to collect the rain,
the falling star sunk in macadam,
summer's last dung beetle, the kiss
of chickweed. Will-o'-the-wisps.

I just moved. Got my current address?

Is there progress? Should I go on
with poesy, this museum, or surrender
to the body, lady? Send me a hint
so I won't be giving you lines
from my poems done up like letters.
Angel, these are images I had left over.

MOVING SOUTH, HE HEARS THIS COLLOQUY INSIDE HIMSELF

If only I spoke, the trees would listen.
Centuries now these oaks have waited, patient
as the fathers of old families underground,
unmoving, rooted in themselves.

Why are you struck dumb
when your tongue should be dancing?

And the birds, too, how shrill they are
at answering, thrushing their brown throats
silver, the underside of song
against my window, before I wake to ask

What did you do, or not,
sleep through, forget, to deserve this?

I have been a man alone before,
winter gathering my face with stubble
in the night I raised a hand to
like a small boy his sex while he's asleep —

why is this moist wind
morning to evening your undoing —

& never felt such silence tightening
my features, my bones closer in the sun
to one another, light shaking like ice
softening but singing this refrain:

Stranger, north or south,
the trees, the birds, the wind
are your mouth. Speak with them.

CODA TO A POETRY READING

I'll try to make this fast.
I know you want to get home,
catch the sports, at least the weather —
it's been good coming here tonight,
packing words to throw through space
neither of us put between us
in this life. Have I come across?

In the midwest — maybe it's different
south? — distance talks to people
through their snowcaps, it says speak alike
or die. We keep our voices low and flat.
We call our children Boredom & Humdrum,
putting her to bed in a backroom,
beating him to his knees for prayers.

I learned there to be afraid of words,
to stand back. Or stay shut up.
I'm trying to find extra syllables
tonight for *Angel, Sparrow, Mother-of-Pearl,
Window.* And now you are leaving —
for *Vertigo, Shadow.* Stranger, don't go yet.
Please, tell me what I've meant.

FROM THE GULF

High summer the clouds here are motionless,
they have nothing to do with us,
the lives we chose. Over the water
they roll back mornings tapering
at their ends, flecked like eggs
a giant sea bird warmed & fled.

And the palms, how quietly they bend
their shafts through white heat, trembling
the upper branches, quivers
in the noon's calm. How strange
at the beach each one of us appears
naked to ourselves & yet a body

Greek deities took on in stone.
While from the surface of the ocean,
at evening, shaking off the foam,
the fixed stars' stare has risen
with their reflections, found their names,
light, light & nothing we can be.

LOCALES

After the last gulls, the scavengers
for Florida shells, the couples leaning
years on each other, after teenagers
leaving the beach the angles of their thighs,
the shark boat shrilling its all clear finally,
the clouds turned, sterns to leeward
across the gulf, a trawl of white fire
stretching to Texas.
                  And there they stood,
two boys straddled by two girls
sexless before adolescence, fully clothed
in black, disguised all afternoon
as shadows on the whitecaps, shallows
of their robes like priests', the full skirts,
long sleeves, swollen, dark with water.
And then they turned, themselves again,
children of the Mennonites, washing me up
on sand still warm before the clouds
lifted, put out to Mexico.

YOU KNOW THIS

The beach is still tonight.
I lie out, my face on the stars,
the sand under my bare back
warm again with noon
& the high tide tourists wade
drowsily up to their rooms
at nightfall & tracks of gulls
stalking this darkness earlier.

I've been waiting, waiting.
Now they have all gone home.
And here, between the Big Dipper
& the Milky Way, like fireworks
from heaven or a tiny rain,
these meteors break the darkness
between my eyes, exploding smoke
as if the sky had somewhere to get to

and I weren't this secret in space
it keeps writing on
with prayers, words overheard
in supermarket check-outs, bars
tongues stand at, thick with dust.
I know you know this,
you, who have passed my way
before, in one of your other lives
& given this poem to me, stranger.

BAYOU AUTUMN

The swans hung over the park
all summer, keeping the sun a flutter
on the lake, the naked bodies
lovers bared each other peddling downstream
in their little boats.
                    And so I turned
inside myself, a stranger to the south,
remembering the snow of swans
molting in another weather.
I grew this skin around my own.

Now in October shadows stir
the lovers' waters. And yet the sun
washes each skin with sweat,
bristling the shore this afternoon
as ice gives way inside me,
my ribs bursting to breathe in
some other air:
                    snow, snow,
the thaw, blood thinning, spring.
And then the light steps through me
hunting for my name, I give it nothing.
I keep myself myself. I watch it go.

And watch the swans sail out
over the lake between the lovers
like clay pigeons to be shot at
by a lonely boy, this distance anywhere
darkness I've carried my whole life
& brought south, missing it till now.

SPIDER

REQUIESCAT

A day will come in my life
when the sky will stop turning an instant,
the fog I have taught myself
to call my name will burn away,
and the prayers where my hands are folded now
will fly off, shooting stars,
to sing again in another tongue.
                                    And then
I will call my soul my soul
without shaking to tell him:
confessor, on nights like this one once
I lived your dare. I went down
into myself and saw the spider
squatting at the center, its eyes mine
and fixed on nothing till I touched it
where it sang and went on singing, singing.
Father, I was not afraid.

THE DESCENT INTO HEAVEN

In New Orleans, the French Market,
it is first light and the farmers' eyes
are still the chain of gold lines lifting
the drive over bayous cool
after midnight, leaving families
in oleander and deep sleep,
the lives of fathers, fathers' fathers, sons.
Their voices buzz, fingering limes, garlic.
They have nothing to land on yet.

Under the stars of summer
tomatoes have squatted, jostling
the slats of trucks, beside squashes
secreting their ripe meat
like the pagan face that shines
through Christ's in medieval paintings
at his last breath, and sugarcane sweating
its white gut and the eggplant
bursting purples of their wounds.

They know what isn't sold
when evening begins to die
with cathedral bells guiding
the tourists to their haunts, the old woman
to her vigil ravening the cans
behind Galatoire's or Brennan's,
will be picked over, squeezed, chosen
to be hurled down, pell-mell, hosed
in the drains for rats and spiders
waiting all day, hairy mouths agog.

This is the descent into heaven:
onions praising the peel of their skins,

the mango its gangrene perfections,
the pear's lung collapsing in laughter,
the thumbprints of peaches dark mouths
as they rise, descend into themselves.
This is how it will be,
the little lights coming on
in all the shops, as they go down,
the night after the last night,
singing, the tourists gaudy flames,
the windows lit up for business,
wishing each other success,
the water dark, the water cold,
goodbye, goodbye, in their new adventures.

AN AFTERMATH

Heaven is this small room
in the middle of winter, my window
the sky holds up to its face
half-shadows, half-sunlight at noon.

Quiet. Absolute quiet.
All night I have struggled to get here,
wrestling him, arms over mine,
tentacles loose at my throat —

and now I have come to myself
with nothing to call my own
but the sound of my own name, this squirming
from that corner I drove him to,

where he'll squat, one eye sleepless
till the next time he appears,
the spider I call my soul,
nights here in the dark, where god comes.

AN EXORCISM

The sky is a dome, it has no sides
to locate, hold him down, no height
his eyes, squinting, can scale.
They stretch its upper reaches, numb:
the sun goes back, goes back, goes back.

He stands facing this, fronting the sea,
the noon. He has walked out quietly
on his life, the house which echoes
with children & his wife. He is nobody now
in the company of so much light.

And this is how it begins, where gulls
swoop & dive, where water breaks
in foam darkening on gills of fish
caught between rocks, then washes out
carrying the shadow of his body —

where he begins wading in, the words
so muted he can't mumble them
to anyone human, the water deepening
black around ankles, knees, his thighs,
his waist, his neck in the yoke of it —

asking the dome to open a crack
the spider inside him might enter
to die, burning to fine, white ash
before he turns back this afternoon —
as if the sun could be done with him, finally.

WITCH BOY

Sometimes, summer nights,
when the world is still,
green, gigantical,

swimming into dawn,
I toss right & left,
while he cries out wild

against my window
Sleeper, come away
from your life, your skin

rotting a body
shaking to the marrow,
laugh off any god,

give my spirit bones,
walk with me tonight
ghostly in the mist,

yourself forever.
I stop up my ears,
steady on my wife,

beside me, my child
he calls his. *Or else*
give me your boy's breath

he whispers, *to bear
up where planets dance
while his body's yours*

till death. Then I wake
cold, sweating that place
he never enters:

rise, shave, shower, dress
putting on the day
for others, others,

the miraculous
vanishing like dew
sucked up by the sun.

SCORPIO

Inside my body a body
waits to be given birth

always, waits for the other
in the heavens to come out:

so in this photograph of myself
the small boy stands

in black swimming suit, black cap
staring up, frowning at noon

before he toddles to the water
to be pulled back, pulling back —

even then it had its sting
rooted, darkening my steps,

poising me on this edge
I move to year by year —

turning me to the fixed light
over my eyes, dimming their stare,

a black spot, cold,
a constellation emptied of stars.

A MAN INHABITED

CALLING

Because I am a man inhabited
my time is before dawn, when light
raises live oaks blue & cold
against the sky like heads of tombs
& the birds are quiet finally
calling each other all night long.

The uniforms of children marching
in unison, the minister's shadow
that paces behind drapes next door
learning his sermon, the old woman
wrapped in muscrat, chenille, veils
to process on her maid's arm —
these inhabitants of the neighborhood
sleep through my rite. I'm hardly here

except to myself, measuring the night
that pours out of my hands
each time I lift them to my eyes.
I try to rub the sleeplessness away.
And now the light is faster
racing between limbs, I hear the mourning dove
singing alone as if inside my head,
wondering why I am chosen
to bear witness to it,
& then be grateful to the dark.

THE NIGHTINGALE

The children have all run home
attended by the first stars
to their tiny, appointed places
under the calls from their mothers,
threats of fathers backed up in town.

Light falls, the last light's mine.
Now that stray cat the children stone
crawls out to listen with me:
the magnolia in full regalia
extends its limbs to sing.

Invisible, the nightingale is there.
Is it possible: only one old tom
& I, preying on darkness, unattached,
catch-as-catch-can, will witness this?
And only I to try to hold it?
More than possible. Knowing I can't.

HOW IT WILL HAPPEN

Later, after supper, I'll go out
into the garden, mute, leaving my wife,
my meat half-cut, the tiny cages
my daughters ring the air with,
canaries perching on a song.

It will be very quiet. My chair,
scraping the terrace like a knife
taking an edge on grindstone,
breaks the silence just a second.
I face the sunset, sit and smoke.

And later still, everyone in bed
behind me, the neighbors' houses hushed
for work tomorrow, darkness fallen
on the sky, I'll put my face out
against the stars. I'll take their pain

from every stump and socket
the constellations have thrown there
and Scorpio, especially, my own.
And then I call them down
still speechless, with this stare

and they'll come, one by one
to sit with me an instant
if I'm lucky like last night
until I find my voice at last
and where they fall the grass will glitter, wet.

MUMMERS

Bodiless, numberless, the days flick by,
figures at the end of my arms,

driving home from work, driving
through paper work numb & abstract

as a map holding one of our smaller wars,
by the trailer court, pushing antennas,

needles, through the sky, gripping
the earth which swells its tanks

flushing somebody's body along,
past a fire that shapes in the dump,

a white hand even at night
beside heads on sticks in their windows,

the propped doll nursing home faces.
I take myself out of myself

to put it back, like this cage
in my skin where blood comes up

to my face, then turns into sleep.
That's almost enough for a life

except for what vanishes
like the head years back of the blind man

who tuned our piano, that sang
from a tunnel between his eyes

white and cracking like fire.
"As if vision might be transfigured

by discipline out of pain," I threw him
once, a conclusion, from the New Criticism

poems & my endings, neat, stuporous
I realize today like the others

I let go, to drive on, remembering.

MAGNOLIA TREE

I

The sky has drawn you out of light
& you sway to it, tensing every branch,
casting the morning at my feet.
Tell me I can approach you
like the squirrels, beyond terror,
having climbed you, & look down.
Tell me my shadow can be yours.

II

Outside my window, in noon heat
I can't bear to enter,
your limbs scream
with jays, the red seeds
they tear at, scattering.
Later, one will sing there.
You have given them your body,
as I would for a song.

III

I cast my soul in darkness
through root, bole, trunk,
stretch upright on the lawn.
At the window my body watches, cold.
And now, as if I were not torn
from you at dawn, we fill with birds.
Come, you are inhabited,
listen with me, know the vanishing.

THE DWARF GARDEN

You who have known the wind
calling from those high places
among rocks where its fingers rest
on the heads of moss, spiders' shadows
or the hawk song vanishing
an instant in blessing
are with me now.
            It is March,
the earth, moist underfoot,
trembles to let me pass
with the wind, loose through the trees,
the calligraphy of the peach,
the apple's tentative flower
it shakes out, a frost on the noon.

You know: even from the gate
live oaks wrap this garden
in their darkness, our eyes squint
to pick them out: the King, the Queen,
the tiny Prince, night around their feet.
These stone dwarves have never seen the sun.

Here, behind a manor house
abandoned to another time,
their single subjects, we have come.
We kneel in the absence of shadow.
We press the cold lips to our own.
You know: the stone eyes glitter, answering.

Later, I will sit among them
where the ground swells, chill, & watch
the first stars break the night sky
& later the dark will take my eyes
& later still our prayer will go out, dark.

LAST CONVERSATION

When I am old, nodding by the fire,
the lamplight turned down low inside my eyes,
come to visit me some night, late.
Just walk in, you'll know how.

I'll grip the chair, speechless at first
to see you, your face floating through the arms
you stretch toward me, burning on yourself.
Speechless, I'll cry. But that will pass.

And we'll have tea, you'll start to talk,
your words swaying up the stairs again
where I first took a step, my hand in yours.
The hall is very dark. I'm not afraid.

Mother, forgive me if I doze off
and don't come back. Just slip away.
Your last words at the banister will be enough
if I should wake up. Even if I don't.

THREE WAKINGS

In first light
I saw the mist
walking in its white robes
down the mountain
running beside my bus,
I touched the damp face
of the window
my reflection kept
all night to itself.
I woke a second time,
tiny on the clear glass
dancing with flame.
I woke again,
stranger to the wrapping
I call my body,
took it on, assumed my name.
And then I was released
to wind among the hills
climbed by stone fences,
wine-dark barns,
farmhouses swimming wheat,
horses racing with the fields —
I sat among these
bowing, radiant
at the feet of light,
the sun opening his hands
to this subject & that.

And what I call the world
rose & took on
the day, accepted it
knowing no other
until the sun had gone
through the skull of the cow
& the holystone stood up
by the roadside with the granite
flashing like teeth
while mist crawled up in the sky
& then the light in us
settled to burn
as I sat back, waiting
for the long, cool shadows of afternoon.

ST. VITUS

When the sun reaches down
under my eyelids
lighting the stones there
that walk me through bracken,
the woods with its tiny
black splutter of flames,
I am transported
swimming grasses' high tides
dividing to lead me
past firs, choir stalls,
where white owl & squirrel
kneel in aisles of ebony light.
I will not come back
as a man, I sing to myself
as if I were asked, *finally*
while the light turns me,
I will be the mist
pausing in the great oaks
before I burn off or this bird
out of sight, ahead,
leading me on, leading me on,
leaving me his song as it vanishes.

AN ARRIVAL

When this night is over
I will go out to the city
with the first light
bearing the gulf wind
standing at bus stops
beside night clerks,
cleaning women & the guards
who punched in yesterday
exhausted, talking softly.

The streets will be white.
When this night is over
they will be washed clean
by my coming, radiant.
I will leave this room
whose windows hold me
locked behind glass
reflecting nothing now
and the shadows of my absence
will not follow.

I will have learned to speak
like a man with himself
in his own language.

And as I leave
the trees will release me,
the birds in the live oaks,
the leaves on every tree,
the quickening in each leaf,
until my hands will open
to tiny creatures
who live, quivering on the air
and I will walk among them
above dragonfly or wasp,
each step an entrance
and the white light stretching
endless under my feet.

SONGS OF THE LOST

MUTE'S SONG

You have not known your own hands
in their minuteness, how the light
tapers evening to them & the sun
flickers on routine business here
lifting cathedrals of stained glass.

You do not know a thing.
Not spoons, not shoes, meeting your voice,
your walk. Not the face in each
radiant as angels. You waste years
talking about talking about talking about that.

But what my eyes touch is me,
shapes itself to mine, reaching out.
Like King Midas' world, I glisten
on all sides, precious, golden.
You also are my skin. I am very fat.

To you, I am the dumb one. Good.
Then come, drop a coin into my cup
rushing to each other, your shadows talking
about love, your poets in love with it.
I don't need even these words.

SONG OF THE IDIOT

I am known by many names.
I have heard you shout them:
Simple, Dimwit, Thick.
Ask me. I can say those back
just like that. Or whisper.
I don't think one is right.

But what you talk about
goes up & down so fast
it is like the little larks
I want to grab & kiss,
to warm in the hollow of my palm.
Do you follow that?

I am a bird without a name
to you, some streak of color
you can't remember. And I am flying
too high, too low. Slowly.
You never see me pass —
why do you laugh, cover your mouth?

You have many names for me.
They are too tight, loose, they scratch.
Every day I try another one on.
If I could wear just one
between my teeth, my shoulder blades
I might cry. Change my color. Molt.

MOTHER'S SONG

I had prepared myself for this,
the night inside my head growing darker,
falling like my breasts, belly, thighs & ass,
announcing that my time is over,
that fields, no matter how long he ploughs,
lie fallow deep inside me here.

But for these losses, what readiness?
To feel each breath contract,
expel & then draw back
one of the eight I brought to life.
They pule like whelps, I labor night & day.
Pain's hands are never off me now.

If God has mercy, if there's God,
after this life I won't bear another.

SONG OF THE OLD MAN

I am almost finished with my pain.
I have raised it in myself for years, each block
a monument upon a monument
until this ceiling spanned the sky
beam by beam, the daylight flickering
like stars dying which finally grew dark.

I sit in it surrounded by the moon
the lust I crave throws over me
& dream that I can dream —
that at my call the women come
when I have made them, that the night
is not my cock, my fingers & my eyes
but a silence I go down on
to never know the other side
or if I'm stiff now. Or awake.

SONG OF THE HOOKER

Since I am alone in the world
& heaven is my destination,
I take them quivering in my mouth,
my ass, flat on my back,
standing, sitting, at every opening.
This is all I ever wanted,
to know the night inside myself
a stranger enters. And my pleasure?
to watch them come & go,
holding God's body inside mine,
shuddering. After this life,
I will know another, then another...

SONG OF THE BLIND MAN

Where I am going now no one can follow me.
It's so narrow I've lit it, wound by wound
with dog teeth I've shaken off, stickweed & yarrow
lining ditches & droppings from the birds
you give those names you can find in books.

I have my own words, silence. My fingers dance.
They answer me, a sort of speech, a song
more rhythmical, softer than your woman's.
While I go down throbbing on the night each noon
your words, stones, graze windows of her room.

I can say: I am what I have touched.
Or: all my waking is so dark, monotonous
it is a prayer. Or: you know surfaces
but not the shadows between them they can keep
for you to fall in. At birth I fell headfirst.

To cross the street, who takes whose arm today.

SONG OF THE SAINT

I'll have to burn this room.
I'll have to pull the stars down
from their appointed places,
stake them, flaming, in your eyes.
And when you charge me, manacling these hands
stigmata steady on themselves,
casting lots for teeth & hair
you'll wear around your necks,
know this:
    thumbs you pressed
through wounds you drove between my ribs
brought down the dark.
      There is a night in me
I tried to spare you, centuries
& soon its face will shine on yours
to sear your flesh
& you will see spiders in that fire
dancing as your souls
time without end & nothing more.

SONG OF THE DROWNED MAN

That figure appeared later
after I was done.
It stood before me
its whole length
burning on itself
& then my spirit rose
taking the air, surrendering
my limbs to float here
among fins of sharks
darkening this water,
all my extremities torn off
as trawlers drag the shore
& in their lifeboats
survivors huddle.

Now I am nothing
but that moment of descent:
my lungs gulping the winds
from Capricorn & Cancer,
drinking the spume
tilted to my lips, turning
the whirlpool's sides,
my cries breaking on the wheel
of seaweed, tiny fishes,
then entering the coral reef,
the bed of shell I knelt in,
seconds.
       The tide is out,
something pulls my bones —
I know — a fish or human voice? —
death swimming in my throat
is all my soul will be
until world's end —
the hooks are lifting me...
that figure dressed in fire,
wherever I am going now
I pray I never see his like again.

SONG OF THE MADMAN

Wonder why I'm always laughing?
Why I'll stop, head-on, throw myself down
into a silence while you're talking
& pound my fists bloody on the floor?
I don't have your excuses, drink
or dope, that job, the girl I should have lost —
I'm no one in the Punch & Judy show
you call a life, while under it your hands,
sticky & white, long to crawl out, naked...
Once I walked & talked. Now I am this stage
I have ceased to visit. No one lights it,
sweeps the wings, lowers & lifts the curtain.
I hacked the seats up, stacked a pyre from the scenes.
And now I am laughing. Quick, laugh with me,
learn how funny somebody else can be.

INFANT'S SONG

Why sing for you?
You're like the little ducks
you hang around my bed, their beaks
your mouths snapping on the air
speckled with shell. Why tell you
beasts I strangled
swimming here, the boles of oaks
that stood aside to let me pass,
how deep the rivers, how many years the rain?
I could sing sea lions languishing
on the dark water, the silence of a wharf
where, between pilings, only the moon listened
to my passing breath, the underside of wings
marsh hawks lifted, white, lighting my way.
Now I am beached
my vision is washed up with your words.
Now, if I could, I would go back.

SONG OF THE HERMIT

Jaybird, do my talking for me.
Say: standing in this room, windows open
on evening scattering the town
with sleep, rich man, poor man,
I am the absence of their dark.

I am the absence of women
abandoned to get here, sing it,
living in my own smell, forgetting
how deep they ran under my hands.
Now I'm half woman. I swim myself.

Louder! The absence of things.
In the minimum I patch rips
like the skyline my eye takes
needle & thread to, a live oak,
bolts of sunlight. I can sew all night.

Little bird, you are that sky
ruffling your wings, your song
props up each corner of my hut.
The silence of crannies, sing! sing!
the loneliest croon to themselves.

I can't let even you in.

THE ROOM WHERE SUMMER ENDS

MOVING AWAY

This mirror has held my breath up
for the last time, the last touch
of April on my window mornings
has chilled to rain. Tomorrow
the floor will sway or level
under another's foot and steady
the dark will gather on me
in a different state, continue knitting
where it stopped.
                    Then I can turn,
casting this house off finally,
my memory loosening each suture
inside my head.
                    Then I can carry it
like any wound healed, superfluous
this life, the next, the next, the next.

WITHIN THE ROOMS OF SUMMER

When you go there, never ask
why am I chosen?
Soon enough shadows call out
your voice & you will walk
with your own, cool, released.
Till then, keep the air
while noon falls from you,
take the shape of nothing
but a dragonfly, oaks swaying
as you pass, bodiless
through the upper branches
to the river, bending.

Today no one looks after you
or knows your touch,
where you came from.
You lay your hands on stones
that they may rise & catch
shadows before they meet —
you who call your soul
into crannies with the slugs
to hear the gods
warming their undersides,
knowing before they speak
such silence finally
as they may leave you.

SKYWRITINGS

There shoud be no one at the end of summer
you'd send a postcard to

about the weather, how it peaks
over the island, building high

a thunderhead of mountains, how the sea
appears to you, dividing

her white skin, evening and the morning,
then leaves you stranded in her shallows,

or how the lizard deepens leaves
with this green sleep or the crab

casts shadows on the bleached sand
ghostlier than snowflakes, scurrying.

No one the mangrove can take in
through roots it lifts like fists

around your dreaming or the starfish
point to, giving up his arms

at the high tide. You keep
the last days to yourself now,

like a man who's dying but knows
how many hours he's got, possessed

by no one, you go on, walking,
walking the water with the water

darkening, the tide out, calm
where the lights in the little boats dim

on the water and go on dimming
the water, dimming and go on.

THE MOUNTAINS

When the mist burns off & the birds
silence their small alarms
outside my window, these appear
or seem to, at the outer edge
of vision. Taking them in,
they are double-double, then my mind's eye
blurs them into clouds
buried in clouds, mirage.
I know I feed the birds each day
because they never asked me to:
simple enough. But these shapes
chill me like tiny children
who flew to my bus window, naked
years ago in an East Texas town,
now this face, now that one, in dreams.

THE RESPONSE

I talk to the rain,
the brother I never had,
while it pounds the window.
I wait for an answer
in a low voice, older than mine.

I've got to know, I say,
how long can I hold on?
why the objects of this room
rise from the floor & walk,
the chair, square dresser, bed,

its white spread ordinary,
the open closet, the fireplace
gaping, shoes emptied of me,
each thing flying away
while my eyes follow them out —

I ask you, why me, here,
this tiny room tonight
high up on a back street,
the sparrow on my ledge
all I spoke to till you came?

I talk on & on
while the rain dies down,

I who waited all evening
for you to drive in
over the mountains, carrying tales

of deer & bear or trout,
the smell of them in your hands.
And now you are leaving,
the room turns, you never were,
& sleep comes & darkness, my answer.

MEDITATIONS AT CRESCENT BEACH

1. The First Prayer

This is where I find myself:
in the eye of the pelican fixed
on nothing, the sky taking his wings,
describing wide arcs, gliding down
over the dark water, hovering.

Or here: where old men come
to squat, high tide around their necks
beside their wives & silent, motionless,
take the undertow, righting themselves.
Steadier, the women draw them in.

And here: the shore beneath my step
releasing the sea into itself.
This is the middle of my life,
I stand at the edge of it, waiting.
Over the low tide evening will come down.

And now: I whisper to him
Soul, fly out of me till morning,
leave my body darkening this water,
then turning home, darkening his bed.
Take me with this word. And I open my lips.

2. The Ecstasy

Quiet of six o'clock in the morning.
Over the gulf's still water
light hovers, shapes itself
to these first birds.
                    Now it rises,
circles wider, gilting pines,
the white sand beach under my feet.

Then, crossing dunes, I'm calling him,
wading shallows with this darkness
I've carried here: soul, soul,
take the form of gull or tern
or pelican — spirit, come down,
let the deep give you my name, surrounding it...

And if you answer, all day sun
will follow me, until I reemerge
through bodies, corridors, the kind of night
no bird ever sees. And if you don't,
later I'm back: ant, mosquito, mite, sand tick —
one of them will take you before dark.

3. The Leavetaking

When I am done with this life
I will come down here
at nightfall, while the tides go out
& they will not return alone.

The rocks will be slippery, black.
Around my ankles will be rainbows
washed up with oil, I will be watched
by fish in it that never stir

except to be cast, washed out,
cast, headless, under my feet.
I will stand very still and wait.
The wind will bring everything to me:

voices huddling windows at my back
light up the dark; the scent of pines
sways like a censer; now the mourning dove
keeps a choir on the air, invisible.

I stand here, facing the sea
where it stretches up touching the sky
& the sky falls quickly to meet it.
I fasten myself to that thin line.

And give my name up, give my face
to the emptiness & hear it answer —
voice, come into the darkness —
& the water is cool about my feet.

THE MISCARRIAGE

There was no talking
about it, the child was here,
the child not a child
followed us through the house
I tried to stay out of.
But in the evening it was there
at the table, refusing food
we had to eat, following the girls
into their game of dolls
till they fought & both cried
over whose was somebody's "baby."
You knew, you knew.
You stayed away from me
& scoured the kitchen sink
where I'd piled plates
in grease while you'd been gone.
You said nothing about it.
It was there at night
drifting about the bedroom
as I tossed in silence
& you did, & neither admitted
we couldn't sleep & I thought
It never had a name.
It had a sex, but what?
The doctors never told us.
It was too little to bury.

And then one evening
it was missing when I got home,
we were talking again
at dinner, the children laughing.
It was not there, not anywhere.
Later, before I dropped off,
I heard a voice certainly
no one's I knew, chanting

The souls of the unborn
wait on an island beyond
the one you will sail for
until the end of time.
Have no pity on us.
We have each other
& know it is better here.
You, too, will think so
when you swim out finally
at world's end & are met by us.

CONFIGURATIONS

All grief is the same.
The crow lands at your window
but you can't feed it enough.
If you could, it would forget you,
join the evening in the lowlands.
It would assume the shapes of firs
going down there, and of giant stones
the earth turns up, too huge,
generations could tell you,
to make that slope
ever fit for plowing.

THE NAMING

I gave my name
to the cold sky
I rose to
& it took it
beyond this room
a second
where the mountain
& horizon meet.
And there it disappeared
among the clouds
blowing in from the north
all morning
so while I worked
I never thought
to call it back.
Waking later
from a nap
mid-afternoon,
I saw the rain
& gave my name,
repeating it,
a chant.
Soon now
I'll have the night sky,
the darkness & the stars
& when I'm done
I'll call them home
to sleep here
assuring them
they go out again
tomorrow.
It has taken me years
to find the things
for my names.
I won't quit now.

ANOTHER AUGUST

In my last life
I stood between oaks like this,
the air tensed, listening
to the trembling of small leaves
cicadas hide in, singing.
Howls. I heard this same dog
far off. Then a screen door
swinging open, Mother's voice
calling me to supper. *Andrew, Andrew—*

I think I put my hand out
here where the lifeline jumps
mornings now in any weather
& touched the lightning once
or twice. The light was deafening.
And then the sun turned & the darkness
that has not lifted since
stepped between me & my life
and the rain which is continuous began to fall.

SONNET

1.... Your tiny fists pray on their own light...
2.... Now they have billowed, white sails
waving your parents goodbye...
3.... They reach out... to the doorknob's handshake...
4.... cat's paw
5.... sweet thumbprint of sweat, they reach through...
6.... the bed in the moon's clenched fist...
7.... the sex of her index finger...
8.... the night's fin of onyx... swimming...
9.... the grasping, the snaking withdrawal... they reach
10.. they reach the roadmap in your child's palm.
11,12,13.... rain, the laying on of its hands
years after year till your bones
are all they can reach for, washing you in —
14.. this shaking at the end of a man...

ANIMA MUNDI

Your last night in the world ·
she will appear from the East, lightning
taking you to her wing,
out of your body, trembling.
This is all you could have asked.

Now at her side you fly,
alight the mountain's peak
giant, to stare down
at cities you never dared to rule
surrendering to smoke. Now the ledge

you never hurled yourself from,
here the mounds of stones
your word never turned to bread.
And then the red air swells
with frogs & locusts in a rain

swaying under you & lakes of fire
where faces surface, tiny fish,
& bodies, headlesss, till you cry
Go back, go back. And then you're home,
your spirit gone, your body alone in your bed.

ARARAT

This is the room where summer ends.
This is the view, a single window
opening to evening: banks of clouds,
shivering to be called down quickly,
step forward, naked, to greet me.

How beautiful each is, assuming
animal form on the lawn
never known before, with beaks & tusks
silver, their feathers, fluttering, gold.
Quivering, they pair off, pair off

till I wonder if the ark has docked tonight
for me. I am not ready yet
though darkness falls from the air
& I have dreamed of this. I've got to pack,
I've got to be wished well by somebody

familiar. The animals are darkening,
calling. They are wading the dark, thrashing.
And now their ivory fetlocks, their horns,
demand an answer going down, *Are you coming*
before the waves close over us, are you.

So. This is my night to leave
carrying nothing, the wind between my eyes,
no one to clear the room of me
or to lie down with me even once.
No one saying the dark is not enough.

CARNEGIE-MELLON POETRY